THUNDER AND LIGHTNING

WENDY PFEFFER

P9-BYJ-136

PHOTO CREDITS: Cover: Keith Kent/Science Photo Library/Photo Researchers, Inc. Page 1: Keith Kent/Peter Arnold, Inc.; 3: Brian Yarvin/Photo Researchers, Inc.; 4: Kenneth W. Fink/Photo Researchers, Inc.; 5: Tony Freeman/PhotoEdit; 6: David M. Grossman/Photo Researchers, Inc.; 7: Lincoln Nutting/Photo Researchers, Inc.; 9: Ron Behrmann/International Stock; 11: Ray Ellis/Photo Researchers, Inc.; 13: Tony Freeman/PhotoEdit; 14: Keith Kent/Peter Arnold, Inc.; 15: Bob Firth/International Stock; 16: Keith Kent/Science Photo Library/Photo Researchers, Inc.; 17: Lionel Brown/The Image Bank; 18: Daniel L. Osborne, University of Alaska/Science Photo Library/Photo Researchers, Inc.; 19: Peter Menzel/Stock Boston; 21: Kent Wood/Photo Researchers, Inc.; 23: Kent Wood/Peter Arnold, Inc.; 24: Virginia Weinland/Photo Researchers, Inc.; 25: Richard Hutchings/PhotoEdit; 27: Bob Krist/Corbis; 28: Gregory K. Scott/Photo Researchers, Inc.; 29: Michael Newman/PhotoEdit; 30: Michael Giannechini/Photo Researchers, Inc.

Library of Congress Cataloging-in-Publication Data available.

ISBN 0-439-42504-2

Book design by Barbara Balch and Kay Petronio
Photo research by Sarah Longacre

10 9 8 7 6 5 4   05 06

Printed in the U.S.A. 23

First trade printing, August 2003

We are grateful to Francie Alexander, reading specialist, and to Adele M. Brodkin, Ph.D., developmental psychologist, for their contributions to the development of this series.

Our thanks also to our science consultants Lee Bennett, PhD, of the University of Washington, Woods Hole Oceanographic Institution, The Franklin Institute, and Drexel University; and Jonathan D. W. Kahl, Professor of Atmospheric Sciences, University of Wisconsin–Milwaukee.

Here comes a storm!

Black **clouds** sweep across
the sky. Strong winds whip
through the trees.

Lightning flashes. **Thunder** crashes. Rain begins to fall. This is a thunderstorm.

How do thunderstorms happen? It takes a few steps for a thunderstorm to form. On hot days, puddles of water dry up. Your wet bathing suit dries, too.

Where does the water go?
It goes up into the clouds.
You cannot see it. But this is
happening all the time.

How does this happen?
Hot air turns water into a
gas you cannot see. This gas is
called **water vapor** (**vay**-pur).

Hot air rises like a balloon. It carries water vapor up to the clouds.

Cold air in the clouds turns the water vapor back into water.

Storm clouds hold billions of drops of water. Some drops join together. They get heavy and fall to Earth as rain.

Winds push the other drops around in the storm clouds. The drops bump into one another.

The bumping causes **static electricity** (**stat**-ik i-lek-**triss**-uh-tee).

You see a flash. You hear a sizzle.

Sometimes, static electricity makes your hair crackle when you comb it.

When electricity starts to flow, it isn't static anymore.

Electricity flows through the air like a river flows on the ground.

This machine makes static electricity.

When electricity flows through
a cloud, a giant **spark** lights up
the sky. This is lightning!

There are many types of
lightning. Some of them are
zigzag, ribbon, ball, and
sheet lightning.

Zigzag lightning follows
two or more paths. It
branches out like the limbs
of a tree.

Ribbon lightning looks
like streamers in the sky.

Red sprite lightning

Astronauts (**as**-truh-nawtz) have seen other types of lightning. These strange glows above thunderstorms have been named blue jets, sprites, and elves.

Blue jets rise from the tops of clouds. Sprites are flashes of red light. Elves are thin rings of light.

Scientists (**sie**-uhn-tistz) are learning what causes these different kinds of lightning. They are studying lightning very carefully both from the earth and from outer space.

Scientists use special rockets to cause lightning.

Every lightning flash makes thunder. How does a flash of light make sound?

As lightning flashes, it heats the air. The hot air pushes out. Then it rushes back.

The hot air pushes out again and rushes back, over and over. This makes the sound you hear. The sound is thunder.

The sound of thunder
travels fast.

But light travels about a
million times faster than
sound. So you *see* lightning
before you *hear* thunder.

Thunder may be scary,
but it cannot hurt you.

Lightning can be dangerous (**dayn**-jur-uhss). It splits trees. It starts fires. Lightning can knock a person off his or her feet. If lightning strikes a person, he or she may be badly hurt.

How can you be safe from lightning during a thunderstorm? Stay in a house or a car. Keep away from open doors and windows. Do not use the telephone, television, computer, or shower.

Don't use the phone during a thunderstorm.

If you are outside, stay away from water, open fields, and trees.

Do not lie down on the ground. Take off any metal, like jewelry.

As the storm moves away, thunder rumbles and rolls.

Lifeguards warn swimmers to leave the water when thunderstorms are in the area.

When the storm stops, the air often feels cool and clean. Puddles, left from the storm, give birds a drink and kids a place to play.

If the sun is shining
after the rain, you may
see a rainbow!

Glossary

clouds—clumps of tiny drops of
water or ice floating in the air

electricity (i-lek-**triss**-uh-tee)—
energy made to flow, either by
natural or human-made activity

lightning—a large spark caused
by electricity traveling in the air

spark—a bright flash of electricity

static (**stat**-ik) **electricity**—energy
that is not moving

thunder—the booming, rumbling
sound that follows a flash of
lightning

water vapor (**vay**-pur)—water
that has been turned into an
invisible gas

A Note to Parents

Learning to read is such an exciting time in a child's life. You may delight in sharing your favorite fairy tales and picture books with your child.

But don't forget the importance of introducing your child to the world of nonfiction. The ability to read and comprehend factual material will be essential to your child in school and throughout life. The Scholastic Science Readers™ series was created especially with beginning readers in mind. These books, with their clear texts and beautiful photographs, will help you to share the wonders of science with *your* new reader.

Suggested Activity

Every lightning flash makes thunder. Did you know there is a way to use lightning and thunder to tell how far away a thunderstorm is? It's simple:

1.) You see lightning before you hear thunder.
2.) Count the seconds between the time you see a lightning flash and the time you hear the thunder.
3.) For each five seconds you count, the storm is 1 mile (2 kilometers) away. For example:

   5 seconds = 1 mile (2 kilometers) away from you
   10 seconds = 2 miles (3 kilometers) away
   15 seconds = 3 miles (5 kilometers) away